Word Puzzles of the Bible from A to Z Word Scrambles

Diane M. Bannard

Bloomington, IN authorHOUSE™ Milton Keynes, UK

AuthorHouse™
1663 Liberty Drive, Suite 200
Bloomington, IN 47403
www.authorhouse.com
Phone: 1-800-839-8640

AuthorHouse™ UK Ltd.
500 Avebury Boulevard
Central Milton Keynes, MK9 2BE
www.authorhouse.co.uk
Phone: 08001974150

First published by AuthorHouse 2/24/2010

ISBN: 978-1-4259-3495-8 (sc)

Printed in the United States of America
Bloomington, Indiana

This book is printed on acid-free paper.

For more information:
P.O. Box 6788
Ocala FL. 34478
352 598-5383
dianemarieba@yahoo.com

Edited by Charles A. Schuman

All scriptures taken from the King James Version Holy Bible

Acknowledgment

I would like to thank all those who had said I could write a book, and two personally: T.E.B. and R.W.K. . I especially want to praise and give thanks very much to my editor Charles A. Schuman. He did a whole lot work and spent so very much time to make this book the very best that he could and much better than I could do without him. I also want to give special recognition and thanks to David R. Tollefson, for his work on the verses and invitational for the book.

dianemarieba@yahoo.com

CONTENTS

INTRODUCTION

All my Puzzle Book verses use the King James Version; because I do all my research in the King James Version.

The Puzzle books are a Bible study motivator not really made as a Bible study, but a fun way to get you into studying the Bible with subject topics. The questions are asked in the way that lets you know how the word applies in the verse. King James Version uses Old English; and are different than we are accustomed to spelling and using some words.

God led me to write the puzzle books to get people more interested in studying the Bible to want to know more about God,. It helps to find interesting ways to learn interpretation of words in the Bible to understand more of what you read. This type of book is really great for young people and newly saved people to get them into reading the Bible and knowing more about God, and is still fun for any one who likes word puzzles of any kind. I hope this book is as enjoyable for you to read as much as it was a pleasure for me to write. I wrote the book so that others could learn to be closer to God and to grow more spiritual and be happier in life

SUBJECT: ABIDE

What is it?

1. To see with attention.   Genesis 19:2
   HOBLED _____

2. To humble yourself to God.   Genesis 22:5
   PIWROSH _____

3. Day of rest.   Exodus 16:29
   BATSABH _____

4. Given an order.   Leviticus 8:35
   DOMANMEDC _____

5. Ceremony of putting on oil.   Numbers 35:25
   NITENADO _____

6. To remain and dwell?   IBEDA _____ Deuteronomy 3:19

7. To desire to find something   I Samuel 22:23
   KETEHES _____

8. To be able to depend on   II Chronicles 32:10
   STURT _____

9. To be alive   GIVINL _____   Jeremiah 10:10

10. Deserving.   Matthew 10:11
    HROTYW _____

11. Put in a certain position.   Mark 6:10
    CAPEL _____

12. Dwelling.   OSUHE _____ Luke 19:5

13. Who is an intercessor?   John 14:16
    ROFETROMC _____

14. Trust in a person   I John 2:28
    DOCEFINECN _____

SUBJECT: BAPTIZED

What is it?

1. Above us.   Matthew 3:16
   SEVANEH _____

2. Ceremoniously immersing a person in   Matthew 20:22
   water. MATBIPS _____

3. A clear liquid.   Mark 1:8
   RAWET_____

4. Freed from sin.   Mark 16:16
   VESAD _____

5. Talk to God   Luke 3:21
   NAGYRIP _____

6. To be righteous.   Luke 7:29
   FEDJISITU _____

7. To have done a task?   Luke 12:50
   CAMPILSODECH _____

8. Followers of Jesus   John 3:22
   LPISEDICS _____

9. Forgiven of a sin   Acts 2:38
   MENOSIRIS _____

10. To have accepted something?   Acts 2:41
    CEVIDERE _____

11. To have trusted.   Acts 8:12
    LEDEVIBE _____

12. To have been in charge.   Acts 8:38
    DONECMADM _____

13. Fully believe.   Acts 16:15
    LATUFIHF _____

14. Taken into baptism.   I Corinthians 12:13
    ZIPETABD _____

SUBJECT: CHOSEN

What is it?

1. To have obtained something.
   NOSEHC _____
   Exodus 14:7

2. Move here.
   MOCE _____
   Numbers 16:5

3. To be unusual.
   CAPELIS _____
   Deuteronomy 7:6

4. Anything.
   TOVEWAHERS _____
   Deuteronomy 12:21

5. Gives testimony.
   SISWETSEN _____
   Joshua 24:22

6. To want strongly.
   RIDESED _____
   I Samuel 12:13

7. To have a group meeting.
   GETACRINOGON _____
   I Chronicles 29:1

8. To be a nation.
   LEPOPE _____
   II Chronicles 6:6

9. To make an agreement.
   NATEVONC _____
   Psalms 89:3

10. A person you like.
    NEFIRD _____
    Isaiah 41:8

11. Favorite selection.
    LETECS _____
    Mark 13:20

12. Complete.
    LEFLUDLIF _____
    John 13:18

13. Those who are sent.
    PASLETOS _____
    Acts 1:2

14. Saved from sin.
    NOTICATSIFINAC _____
    II Thessalonians 2:13

15. A kind of offspring.
    NERAGOTENI _____
    I Peter 2:9

SUBJECT: DREAM

What is it?

1. A messenger.   NALEG _____   Genesis 31:11
2. To have imagined.   Genesis 37:5
   MERADED _____
3. Get the meaning   Genesis 41:15
   NSADUDNETR _____
4. Seen in the mind.   Numbers 12:6
   SONIVI _____
5. Just came into sight.   I Kings 3:5
   PAREDAPE _____
6. To be asleep.   Job 33:15
   LNEMSIRSUGB _____
7. Arisen.   Psalms 73:20
   WASAKET _____
8. It is dark.   Isaiah 29:7
   GTIHN _____
9. To imagine. REMAD _____   Jeremiah 23:28
10. Spiritual explanation.   Daniel 2:6
    TIPARINETORENT _____
11. Let it be known.   Matthew 2:12
    NDERAW _____
12. Tell what will happen.   Acts 2:17
    RHOYPEPS _____

4

SUBJECT: ENDURE

What is it?

1. To go by.   SAPS _____   Genesis 33:14

2. What is one begotten of?   Esther 8:6
   DRINEDK _____

3. An upright position.   Job 8:15
   DTASN _____

4. Be ready.   Psalms 9:7
   REDAPPER _____

5. To remain.   Psalms 30:5
   TUREDEHN _____

6. In every age.   Psalms 72:5
   GUHOTUROTH _____

7. Perpetuated.   Psalms 72:17
   DOTINUNEC _____

8. A recalling of the past.   Psalms 102:12
   BEMARCEMENR_____

9. To be mighty.   Ezekiel 22:14
   TSONGR _____

10. Be made whole   Matthew 24:13
    DAVES _____

11. To last.   Mark 13:13
    DERUNE _____

12. To wait.   II Thessalonians 1:4
    CENIPETA _____

13. Show evidence of   II Timothy 4:5
    FOPOR _____

14. A feeling of joy.   James 5:11
    PAPYH _____

SUBJECT: FAVOUR

What is it?

1. Have praised.   Genesis 30:27
   LESDESB _____
2. Important. TEGAR _____   Exodus 11:3
3. Steadily calm.   Deuteronomy 28:50
   TACENOCNUNE _____
4. Meet the need.   Deuteronomy 33:23
   TIFADESIS _____
5. Appointed.   Joshua 11:20
   DANCEMODM _____
6. To attain.   I Samuel 16:22
   NOFUD _____
7. Try to get.   Esther 2:17
   NADOTEBI _____
8. Very pleasant.   Esther 8:5
   LIPASEGN _____
9. Care.   Job 10:12
   SITANITIVO _____
10. A feeling of satisfaction.   Psalms 102:14
    SERALEPU _____
11. The part that feels love.   Psalms 119:58
    RETAH _____
12. On your side.   Proverbs 19:6
    REDFIN _____
13. To serve others.   Isaiah 60:10
    SIREMINT _____
14. Help another.   Jeremiah 16:13
    VAFORU _____
15. Much caring.   Daniel 1:9
    VELO _____
16. A being that lives in heaven.   Luke 1:30
    NELAG _____
17. Wanted.   Acts 7:46
    REDISED _____

SUBJECT: GREAT

What is it?

1. Very important.   Genesis 12:2
   RATEG _____

2. To have much respect.   Numbers 24:11
   NOHURO _____

3. To make glad.   I Kings 1:40
   JOCIREDE _____

4. Spoken an approval.   I Chronicles 16:25
   RASIPED _____

5. A great supply.   II Chronicles 9:9
   DUNACANEB _____

6. Many were pleased.   Nehemiah 8:17
   DLANSESG _____

7. Very glorious. TEJYSAM _____   Psalms 21:5

8. Thoughts in sleep. MERAD _____   Daniel 2:6

9. Given for something done well.   Matthew 5:12
   WADRER_____

10 To have total trust in something   Matthew 15:28
   TIHAF _____

11. A pastor.   RISETINM_____   Matthew 20:26

12. A law of the Bible.   Matthew 22:36
    MNOCDEMTANM _____

13. To gather a crop.   Luke 10:2
    RAHSETV _____

14. To be righteous. FIJISUDET _____   I Timothy 3:16

15. To rescue.   Hebrews 2:3
    NAVASILOT _____

16. People giving evidence.   Hebrews 12:1
    TENSEWSIS _____

SUBJECT: HOLINESS

What is it?

1. To give a good opinion of something.   Exodus 15:11
   SISERAP _____

2. Nothing added.   RUPE _____   Exodus 28:36

3. To give great praise. ROLYG _____   I Chronicles 16:29

4. Makes something pleasant.   II Chronicles 20:21
   TAYUBE _____

5. Being consecrated.   II Chronicles 31:18
   TANCIFESID _____

6. Done during church service.   Psalms 29:2
   RSOPHIW _____

7. A King does   NETIGERH _____   Psalms 47:8

8. Mighty.   REGAT _____   Psalms 48:1

9. Done when happy.   JICEROE _____   Psalms 60:6

10. Declarations.   Psalms 93:5
    MONISETISET _____

11. Ability to do something. WEROP _____ Psalms 110:3

12. Our sky.   EVAHEN _____   Isaiah 63:15

13. The main room for service.   Isaiah 63:18
    TASRANYUC _____

14. The very beginnings.   Jeremiah 2:3
    TRUFRISTIFS _____

15. A reward or punishment.   Jeremiah 31:23
    CITUSEJ   _____

16. Future times.   Amos 4:2
    TIRESTYOP _____

17. Virtuousness.   Luke 1:75
    TOREGHUSNISES _____

18. Never ending.   Romans 6:22
    VLITARNESEG _____

19. Cause to hope.   II Corinthians 7:1
    MOSIPERS   _____

20. Enjoyment.   LASUPERE _____   Hebrews 12:10

SUBJECT: INCREASE

What is it?

1. Very great.   Deuteronomy 6:3
   GYHITMIL _____

2. One tenth of one's income.   Deuteronomy 14:28
   HITET _____

3. Have a start   Job 8:7
   GNENGIBIN_____

4. Mighty acts.   Psalms 71:21
   NEGSATSER _____

5. Gaining knowledge.   Proverbs 1:5
   RINEGNAL_____

6. Multiplied.   Ecclesiastes 5:11
   CASENEDIR _____

7. Carry out something?   Isaiah 9:7
   FEMROPR _____

8. To make less.   John 3:30
   SECEDARE _____

9. Grow.   I Corinthians 3:6
   NICERESA _____

10. To have a large amount.   I Thessalonians 3:12
    BONADU _____

SUBJECT: JERICHO

What is it?

1. A person of special rank.   Numbers 26:3
   SITEPR _____
2. Part of the family.   Numbers 26:63
   DRICHENL _____
3. Clear areas.   Numbers 33:50
   NIPALS _____
4. Something you can get.   Numbers 34:15
   TIHIRECENAN _____
5. Lives in a certain place.   Joshua 9:3
   TABANSITHIN _____
6. To give out in shares.   Joshua 13:32
   TIRBUDSITE _____
7. All the people living together.   Joshua 18:21
   MALEFISI _____
8. Once a leader.   I Kings 16:34
   HUJOSA _____
9. Made by putting together.   Nehemiah 3:2
   DULEDIB _____
10. A great city   Jeremiah 52:8
    RECIJOH _____
11. Large crowd.   Matthew 20:29
    TUMITEDUL _____
12. Human beings.   Mark 10:46
    POPELE _____
13. Gone in.   Luke 19:1
    NETEDER _____
14. Encircled.   Hebrews 11:30
    MASDECOPS _____

SUBJECT: KINDNESS

What is it?

1. To have decided upon.   Genesis 24:14
   WHEDES _____

2. Show graciously.   Judges 8:35
   SNODEGOS _____

3. Be fortunate.   Ruth 2.20
   SEDLEBS _____

4. People who help one another. II Samuel 3:8
   DRIFENS_____

5. Honesty.   I Kings 3:6
   TENSIPSGUHR _____

6. Kindness.   Nehemiah 9:17
   CORISUGA _____

7. Satisfied.   Esther 2:9
   SADEPEL_____

8. Causing wonder.   Psalms 31:21
   LESOMURALV _____

9. To worship.   Psalms 117:2
   ERIPAS _____

10. A sincere request to God. Psalms 141:5
    RYAPER_____

11. Perform the part of Mediator. Isaiah 54:8
    EDEMERER _____

12. Show mercy   Jeremiah 2:2
    SDINKESN _____

13. Forgiving.   Joel 2:13
    FIMURECL _____

14. Exceedingly. REGAT _____ Jonah 4:2

15. Cleanness.   II Corinthians 6:6
    SNUREPES _____

15. To be patient. KENESEMS _____ Colossians 3:12

17. One that rescues. IRAVOSU _____ Titus 3:4

18. Faithful in worship.   II Peter 1:7
    LOGIDSNES _____

SUBJECT: LOVE

What is it?
1. Another person, near you.   Leviticus 19:18
    BONEGIRUH _____
2. Great strength.   THIGM _____ Deuteronomy 6:5
3. To have deliverance.   Psalms 40:16
    LATIVOSAN _____
4. With no end.   Jeremiah 31:3
    RVALISENETG_____
5. Great respect.   RUNOHO _____Matthew 19:19
6. Law of the Bible.   Mark 12:31
    NMETMACNOMD _____
7. Center of feelings.   TERAH _____Luke 10:27
8. To have more.   RATERGE_____John 15:13
9. Cooperate.   GETOHRET _____ Romans 8:28
10. Kindness.   Galatians 5:22
    NETGELSENS _____
11. A pleasing quality.   REGAC _____Ephesians 6:24
12. Obtained by studying.   Philippians 1:9
    NOLEGKEDW_____
13. A belief in God   TAHIF _____I Thessalonians 5:8
14. Justice.   II Timothy 4:8
    SNETHOGISURES _____
15. To be friendly.   Hebrews 13:1
    LBOTREHYR _____
16. Exalt.   ECIROJE _____I Peter 1:8
17. To be dear.   DELOBEV _____ I John 4:7
18. Have affection for   VOLE _____Revelations 3:19

12

SUBJECT: MULTIPLY

What is it?

1. When you grow.   Genesis 1:22
    LITUFURF _____

2. Happened on your birthday.   Genesis 6:1
    NORB _____

3. To bring forth greatly.   Genesis 8:17
    DUBLANYTAN _____

4. To furnish again.   Genesis 9:1
    PERLESHIN _____

5. Have brought in an increase.   Genesis 9:7
    RTOFH _____

6. A crowd of people.   Genesis 28:3
    DULITEMUT _____

7. Take as a heritage.   Exodus 32:13
    TINIHER _____

8. Confirm.   TELABSHIS _____   Leviticus 26:9

9. Get plenty.   PITELUDIML_____   Deuteronomy 8:13

10. Get exceedingly.   Deuteronomy 17:17
    TYGELAR _____

11. Received abundantly.   Deuteronomy 30:16
    LSESB _____

12. Increase.   LPIMYLUT _____   Job 29:18

13. Show you are grateful.   Jeremiah 30:19
    TGANSINGIHVK _____

14. Show a great amount.   Jeremiah 33:22
    SEREMADU _____

15. First actions.   Ezekiel 36:11
    NGINBISNEG _____

16. To produce.   Ezekiel 36:30
    CARESENI _____

17. Planter.   ROWES _____   II Corinthians 9:10

18. Cause to abound.   Hebrews 6:14
    YLPINTUMGIL _____

SUBJECT: NEIGHBOUR

What is it?

1. Your home is a...   Exodus 12:4
   SULEHODOH   _____

2. A testimony. NETSIWS _____   Exodus 20:16

3. To transfer. VEDIREL _____   Exodus 22:10

4. Gets along with others.   Exodus 32:27
   NOPACINOM _____

5. To be just.   Leviticus 19:15
   TEROSIGSEHUNS _____

6. A friend. BIROGUNEH _____   Deuteronomy 23:25

7. Become right. MEGINEDER _____   Ruth 4:7

8. Place of spiritual rule.   I Samuel 15:28
   GINKOMD _____

9. People who tell what will happen.   I Kings 20:35
   HREPTOPS _____

10. Ridicule. DEGAHUL _____   Job 12:4

11. Mixed feelings. TERAH _____   Psalms 12:2

12. To be aware of.   Proverbs 11:9
    LEKODWEGN _____

13. Ability to be contented. YPAPH _____   Proverbs 14:21

14. Sign of respect.   Isaiah 3:5
    BANORELUHO _____

15. Able to control ones fear.   Isaiah 41:6
    OGARECU _____

16. Most noble. TASEGERT _____   Jeremiah 31:34

17. Giving up something.   Mark 12:33
    CESIFACISR _____

18. Ability to last. GRTESHTN_____   Luke 10:27

19. Complete contentment.   Romans 13:10
    LIFINILGULF _____

20. Written of the Bible.   James 2:8
    TISRUCEPR_____

SUBJECT: OBSERVE

What is it?

1. An Era.   Exodus 12:17
    RENAGITESON _____

2. A custom. NIDECORAN_____   Exodus 12:24

3. Doing of worship by Christians.   Exodus 31:16
    TABHASB _____

4. Its best quality.   Exodus 34:22
    TRUTFIFSISR _____

5. Rules.   Leviticus 19:37
    TETUSATS_____

6. To give an order   Numbers 28:2
    MODMACN _____

7. Caused to hope   Deuteronomy 6:3
    SODIPERM _____

8. To give as proof.   Deuteronomy 32:46
    FESITYT _____

9. Saints are thought to go here.   Nehemiah 1:5
    VENAHE _____

10. Mercifulness.   Psalms 107:43
    VKESNDINOLGINS _____

11. To be guided.   Proverbs 23:26
    SOREVEB _____

12. Providing knowledge and training. Matthew 28:20
    CINEGTAH_____

13. To suppose.   Acts 21:25
    ELEVIBE _____

SUBJECT: PARABLE

What is it?

1. A mass of people.   Numbers 24:20
   TOSINAN _____

2. To have said more of.   Job 29:1
   NOTIDUCEN _____

3. Commonly said.   Psalms 49:4
   SYINAG _____

4. A simple story with a moral meaning.   Proverbs 26:7
   RABELAP _____

5. Puzzling problem requiring clever solution.   Ezekiel 17:2
   DLIRED _____

6. Old saying of wisdom.   Habakkuk 2:6
   VOBRERP _____

7. Realm.   Matthew 13:24
   DOGMINK_____

8. A crowd.   Matthew 13:34
   DELITUTUM_____

9. Followers of Jesus. CISPELSID_____ Mark 4:34

10. Said aloud.   Mark 12:12
    KOSPEN_____

11. A great amount.   Luke 12:16
    FLINTELYLUP_____

12. To present oneself.   Luke 19:11
    PERAPA _____

SUBJECT: QUEEN

What is it?

1. To have received sound.   I Kings 10:1
    RADEH_____

2. Good sense.   I Kings 10:4
    DISMOW _____

3. A lot of goods.   I Kings 10:10
    DECUBANAN _____

4. The king of a kingdom is...   I Kings 10:13
    LOYAR _____

5. A kind action. VUFORA _____   I Kings 11:19

6. A mistress of a kingdom.   I Kings 15:13
    ENUQE _____

7. Fellow members.   II Kings 10:13
    HRETBENR _____

8. A group joined together in some work.   II Chronicles 9:1
    POCYMAN_____

9. To be much loved.   II Chronicles 9:9
    COSIPERU _____

10. Having to do with something.   II Chronicles 15:16
    NONGECNICR_____

11. Feeling of gotten something desired.   Nehemiah 2:6
    LESADEP _____

12. Things that makes it pleasant to think   Esther 1:11
    about. ATEYUB _____

13. To dress.   Esther 4:4
    THELOC _____

14. Headdress of gold.   Jeremiah 13:18
    WRONC _____

15. To take one thing in place of another.   Daniel 5:10
    HDENCAG _____

SUBJECT: REDEEM

What is it?

1. Oldest child.   Exodus 13:13
   BSIFRONTR _____

2. Thing given up.   Exodus 13:15
   CIFERISAC _____

3. Something seized.   Leviticus 25:25
   SPESONISOS _____

4. Be very holy.   Leviticus 27:19
   FIDENTICAS _____

5. To be free.   Numbers 18:16
   DEREDEME _____

6. Purchase.   Ruth 4:4
   EDEREM _____

7. Something gained.   Ruth 4:6
   TINECHARINE _____

8. People sharing the same history.   II Samuel 7:23
   TANONIS_____

9. People hired for a cause.   Nehemiah 5:5
   NVERSAST _____

10. To rescue.   Job 6:23
    LEVIRED _____

11. To be trustworthy.   Psalms 26:11
    GETINTIRY _____

12. Reserve.   Psalms 49:15
    ICEVERE _____

13. Too delicate.   Psalms 72:14
    CESOPIRU _____

14. To be sorry.   Hosea 13:14
    TEPNACEREN _____

15. To choose unto ones family.   Galatians 4:5
    DIPONATO _____

16. To make clean.   Titus 2:14
    RIFUPY _____

SUBJECT: SAVED

What is it?

1. To be fortunate. PAPYH _____ Deuteronomy 33:29
2. To preserve. LIVEREDED _____ II Samuel 19:9
3. A very important person. II Samuel 22:4
   HROTYW _____
4. To have strength.   HTIMYG _____ Psalms 106:8
5. Eternal. LESTIVEGANR _____ Isaiah 45:17
6. Justice. Jeremiah 23:6
   SETIGSOSNERUH _____
7. Have caused to feel great. Matthew 19:25
   ZADEMA _____
8. To have surprised. Mark 10:26
   TONISHADES _____
9. To have picked out.   HESONC _____ Luke 23:35
10. The Earth and its people. John 3:17
    ROLWD _____
11. Safety. LASTONAVI _____ Acts 4:12
12. A feeling that what one wants will Romans 8:24
    happen. OPEH _____
13. A sincere request.   YERAPR _____ Romans 10:1
14. To have kept from harm. VADES _____ I Corinthians 3:15
15. Messiah. STIRCH _____ II Corinthians 2:15
16. God's gift. RACEG _____ Ephesians 2:8
17. Discernment. I Timothy 2:4
    LENDEKWOG _____
18. Rational beings.   LUSOS _____ I Peter 3:20
19. A lamp.   TGIHL _____ Revelation 21:24

19

SUBJECT: TITHES

What is it?

1. Full of bliss.   Genesis 14:20
   LESBESD _____

2. To pay off.   Leviticus 27:31
   DEMERE _____

3. To gain a possession.   Numbers 18:24
   RENECANITIH _____

4. Slaughtered animals.   Deuteronomy 12:6
   CERISIFASC _____

5. An addition.   Deuteronomy 26:12
   RESECINA _____

6. Something loved.   Nehemiah 10:38
   SERATERU _____

7. To have gladness.   Nehemiah 12:44
   JOCIREDE _____

8. Increase.   Amos 4:4
   PUTILYML _____

9. Oblations.   Malachi 3:8
   SFERIGONF _____

10. Paradise.   Malachi 3:10
    NEHAVE _____

11. Something that belongs to one.   Luke 18:12
    SPSESOS _____

12. The law God gave to Moses.   Hebrews 7:5
    MCATMENMODN_____

13. Pledges.   Hebrews 7:6
    MESIPOSR _____

14. A tenth part.   Hebrews 7:8
    TEHITS _____

SUBJECT: UPRIGHTNESS

What is it?

1. Correctness.   Deuteronomy 9:5
   NOSGISEHUSRET _____

2. Appointed.   I Kings 9:4
   MODECMADN _____

3. Favourable.   I Chronicles 29:17
   LESAREPU _____

4. Trust...   Job 4:6
   NIFEDECONC _____

5. Wittingly.   Job 33:3
   NELGEDOWK _____

6. Contend.   Psalms 9:8
   NETISIMR _____

7. Keep in a certain condition.   Psalms 25:21
   SEVERPER _____

8. Fact.   THURT _____   Psalms 111:8

9. A mind.   REHAT _____   Psalms 119:7

10. A state of mind.   RITSIP _____   Psalms 143:10

11. Honesty.   Proverbs 14:2
    HPIGTERSUSN _____

12. Have more worth.   Proverbs 28:6
    TERETB _____

13. Straight up and down.   Isaiah 26:7
    PIGHUTR _____

14. Stateliness.   Isaiah 26:10
    JETYMAS _____

SUBJECT: VICTORY

What is it?

1. Excellent   II Samuel 23:10
   RATEG _____

2. To be praised.   I Chronicles 29:11
   LEXADET_____

3. To be splendid.   Psalms 98:1
   LEROMULASV _____

4. The ground.   Isaiah 25:8
   RATEH _____

5. The way of justice.   Matthews 12:20
   MDUGTEJN _____

6. To show gratefulness   I Corinthians 15:57
   KNASHT _____

7. To get the better of.   I John 5:4
   TEMHORECOV _____

8. The winning of battle.   Revelations 15:2
   CITYOVR _____

SUBJECT: WILLING

What is it?

1. To go after.   Genesis 24:5
   LOWLOF _____

2. No matter what person.   Exodus 35:5
   SOREWEHOV _____

3. A consent. TAREHED _____   Exodus 35:22

4. A gift. RONEFGIF _____   Exodus 35:29

5. Past tense of think.   I Chronicles 28:9
   HTUGHOST _____

6. Ministering   I Chronicles 28:21
   REVECIS _____

7. Ready to do something.   Job 39:9
   LINWIGL _____

8. Sanctuary. SLONIHES _____   Psalms 110:3

9. To try diligently.   Isaiah 1:19
   DENIBETO_____

10. Intended. DENDIM _____   Matthew 1:19

11. Handed over.   Mark 15:15
    RIDEVELED _____

12. To show to be fair.   Luke 10:29
    FUSYJIT _____

13. Great joy. ECOJIRE _____   John 5:35

14. The reason for something.   Acts 27:43
    SOPUPER _____

15. To last. DERUNED _____   Romans 9:22

16. To be bold.   II Corinthians 5:8
    TIFNODECN _____

17. To transmit.   I Timothy 6:18
    NUCOMITEMAC _____

18. Divine assurance.   Hebrews 6:17
    MOSIPER _____

19. Really true.   Hebrews 13:18
    NLOSHETY _____

23

SUBJECT X) EXCELLENT:

1. greatness   Esther 1:4
   JASETYM_____

2. the absolute power   Job 37:23
   THALYGIM_____

3. firmaments   Psalms 8:1
   NESAVEH_____

4. mercifulness   Psalms 36:7
   SNEGLONSIDNIKV_____

5. magnificent   Psalms 76:4
   IROSULOG_____

6. celebrate   Psalms 150:2
   SEPARI_____

7. shiny   Daniel 2:31
   GRESHBTISN_____

8. reputation   Daniel 4:36
   ROHUNO_____

9. pure   Philippians 1:10
   CIRENES_____

10. glorious   Hebrews 1:4
    CENTEXLEL_____

11. service   Hebrews 8:6
    STINYMIR_____

12. dear   II Peter 1:17
    DOVEBEL_____

24

SUBJECT: YIELD

What is it?

1. Advanced gain.   Leviticus 19:25
   CERASENI _____

2. A wide piece of country land.   Leviticus 26:4
   LIDEF _____

3. Parts of certain plants.   Deuteronomy 11:17
   TURIF_____

4. To bring happiness.   LSEBS _____   Psalms 67:6

5. To root.   Psalms 107:37
   NPALT _____

6. To give up. LYIDE _____   Proverbs 7:21

7. Where grapes grow.   Isaiah 5:10
   YEVARIDN _____

8. To preserve.   Ezekiel 34:27
   LIDEREVED _____

9. Tempest.   Hosea 8:7
   RHIWDINLW_____

10. Pleasant place.   Joel 2:22
    TUSERAPS_____

11. Solid part of the land's surface.   Mark 4:8
    NODGUR_____

12. A vow.   TOHA _____   Acts 23:21

13. Used to get something done.   Romans 6:13
    MNISTUSTERN _____

14. Submissive.   Romans 6:16
    EDIBENOCE _____

25

SUBJECT: ZEAL

What is it?

1. Left over.   II Samuel 21:2
   NTEMRAN _____

2. To sit on and move along.   II Kings 10:16
   DERI _____

3. To defy or cause shame.   Psalms 69:9
   CAROHEPERS _____

4. Grouped letters which having meaning.   Psalms 119:139
   SWORD _____

5. To carry out.   Isaiah 9:7
   FERPOMR _____

6. Soldiers.   Isaiah 37:32
   TSOSH _____

7. Any piece of clothing.   Isaiah 59:17
   RTEMSAGN _____

8. The quality of being strong.   Isaiah 63:15
   TSHERTNG _____

9. To ease one's pain.   Ezekiel 5:13
   TERMOCODF _____

10. Eagerness.   John 2:17
    LAZE _____

11. To write down for future use.   Romans 10:2
    CEDROR _____

12. Feel favourable towards.   II Corinthians 7:11
    DOPREVAP_____

13. Determination.   II Corinthians 9:2
    NDOFRARSESW_____

14. Religious congregation   Phiippians 3:6
    HCRUHC _____

Genesis 1:22
And God blessed them, saying, Be fruitful, and multiply, and fill the waters in the seas, and let fowl multiply in the earth.

Genesis 6:1
And it came to pass, when men began to multiply on the face of the earth, and daughters were born unto them,

Genesis 8:17
Bring forth with thee every living thing that is with thee, of all flesh, both of fowl, and of cattle, and of every creeping thing that creepeth upon the earth; that they may breed abundantly in the earth, and be fruitful, and multiply upon the earth.

Genesis 9:1
And God blessed Noah and his sons, and said unto them, Be fruitful, and multiply, and replenish the earth.

Genesis 9:7
And you, be ye fruitful, and multiply; bring forth abundantly in the earth, and multiply therein.

Genesis 12:2
And I will make of thee a great nation, and I will bless thee, and make thy name great; and thou shalt be a blessing:

Genesis 14:20
And blessed be the most high God, which hath delivered thine enemies into thy hand. And he gave him tithes of all.

Genesis 19:2
And he said, Behold now, my lords, turn in, I pray you, into your servant's house, and tarry all night, and wash your feet, and ye shall rise up early, and go on your ways. And they said, Nay; but we will abide in the street all night.

Genesis 22:5
And Abraham said unto his young men, Abide ye here with the ass; and I and the lad will go yonder and worship, and come again to you.

Genesis 24:5
And the servant said unto him, Peradventure the woman will not be willing to follow me unto this land: must I needs bring thy son again unto the land from whence thou camest?

Genesis 24:14
And let it come to pass, that the damsel to whom I shall say let down thy pitcher, I pray thee, that I may drink, and she shall say drink and I will give thy camels drink also: let the same be she that thou hast appointed for thy servant Isaac: and thereby shall I know that thou hast shewed kindness unto my maser

Genesis 28:3
And God Almighty bless thee, and make thee fruitful, and multiply thee, that thou mayest be a multitude of people;

Genesis 30:27
And Laban said unto him, I pray thee, if I have found favour in thine eyes, tarry: for I have learned by experience that the LORD hath blessed me for thy sake.

Genesis 31:11
And the angel of God spake unto me in a dream, saying, Jacob: And I said, Here am I.

Genesis 33:14
Let my lord, I pray thee, pass over before his servant: and I will lead on softly, according as the cattle that goeth before me and the children be able to endure, until I come unto my lord unto Seir.

Genesis 37:5
And Joseph dreamed a dream, and he told it his brethren: and they hated him yet the more.

Genesis 41:15
And Pharaoh said unto Joseph, I have dreamed a dream, and there is none that can interpret it: and I have heard say of thee, that thou canst understand a dream to interpret it.

Exodus 11:3
And the LORD gave the people favour in the sight of the Egyptians. Moreover the man Moses was very great in the land of Egypt, in the sight of Pharaoh's servants, and in the sight of the people.

Exodus 12:4
And if the household be too little for the lamb, let him and his neighbour next unto his house take it according to the number of the souls; every man according to his eating shall make your count for the lamb.

Exodus 12:17
And ye shall observe the feast of unleavened bread; for in this selfsame day have I brought your armies out of the land of Egypt: therefore shall ye observe this day in your generations by an ordinance for ever.

Exodus 12:24
And ye shall observe this thing for an ordinance to thee and to thy sons for ever.

Exodus 13:13
And every firstling of an ass thou shalt redeem with a lamb; and if thou wilt not redeem it, then thou shalt break his neck: and all the firstborn of man among thy children shalt thou redeem.

Exodus 13:15
And It came to pass, when Pharaoh would hardly let us go, that the LORD slew all the firstborn in the land of Egypt, both the firstborn of man, and the firstborn of beast: therefore I sacrifice to the LORD all that openeth the matrix, being males; but all the firstborn of my children I redeem.

Exodus 14:7
And he took six hundred chosen chariots, and all the chariots of
Egypt, and captains over every one of them.

Exodus 15:11
Who is like unto thee, O LORD, among the gods? who is like thee,
glorious in holiness, fearful in praises, doing wonders?

Exodus 16:29
See, for that the LORD hath given you the sabbath, therefore he
giveth you on the sixth day the bread of two days; abide ye every man
in his place, let no man go out of his place on the seventh day.

Exodus 20:16
Thou shalt not bear false witness against thy neighbour.

Exodus 22:10
If a man deliver unto his neighbour an ass, or an ox, or a sheep, or
any beast, to keep; and it die, or be hurt, or driven away, no man
seeing it:

Exodus 28:36
And thou shalt make a plate of pure gold, and grave upon it, like the
engravings of a signet, HOLINESS TO THE LORD.

Exodus 31:16
Wherefore the children of Israel shall keep the sabbath, to observe the
sabbath throughout their generations, for a perpetual covenant.

Exodus 32:13
Remember Abraham, Isaac, and Israel, thy servants, to whom thou
swarest by thine own self, and saidst unto them, I will multiply your
seed as the stars of heaven, and all this land that I have spoken of will
I give unto your seed, and they shall inherit it for ever.

Exodus 32:27
And he said unto them, Thus saith the LORD God of Israel, Put
every man his sword by his side, and go in and out from gate to gate
throughout the camp, and slay every man his brother, and every man
his companion, and every man his neighbour.

Exodus 34:22
And thou shalt observe the feast of weeks, of the firstfruits of wheat
harvest, and the feast of ingathering at the year's end.

Exodus 35:5
Take ye from among you an offering unto the LORD: whosoever is
of a willing heart, let him bring it, an offering of the LORD; gold,
and silver, and brass,

Exodus 35:22
And they came, both men and women, as many as were willing
hearted, and brought bracelets, and earrings, and rings, and tablets,
all jewels of gold: and every man that offered offered an offering of
gold unto the LORD.

Exodus 35:29
The children of Israel brought a willing offering unto the LORD,
every man and woman, whose heart made them willing to bring for
all manner of work, which the LORD had commanded to be made
by the hand of Moses.

Leviticus 8:35
Therefore shall ye abide at the door of the tabernacle of the
congregation day and night seven days, and keep the charge of the
LORD, that ye die not: for so I am commanded.

Leviticus 19:15
Ye shall do no unrighteousness in judgment: thou shalt not respect
the person of the poor, nor honor the person of the mighty: but in
righteousness shalt thou judge thy neighbour.

Leviticus 19:18
Thou shalt not avenge, nor bear any grudge against the children of thy people, but thou shalt love thy neighbour as thyself: I am the LORD.

Leviticus 19:25
And in the fifth year shall ye eat of the fruit thereof, that it may yield unto you the increase thereof: I am the LORD your God.

Leviticus 19:37
Therefore shall ye observe all my statutes, and all my judgments, and do them: I am the LORD.

Leviticus 25:25
If thy brother be waxen poor, and hath sold away some of his possession, and if any of his kin come to redeem it, then shall he redeem that which his brother sold.

Leviticus 26:4
Then I will give you rain in due season, and the land shall yield her increase, and the trees of the field shall yield their fruit

Leviticus 26:9
For I will have respect unto you, and make you fruitful, and multiply you, and establish my covenant with you.

Leviticus 27:19
And if he that sanctified the field will in any wise redeem it, then he shall add the fifth part of the money of thy estimation unto it, and it shall be assured to him.

Leviticus 27:31
And if a man will at all redeem ought of his tithes, he shall add thereto the fifth part thereof.

Numbers 12:6
And he said, Hear now my words: If there be a prophet among you,
I the LORD will make myself known unto him in a vision, and will
speak unto him in a dream.

Numbers 16:5
And he spake unto Korah and unto all his company, saying, Even to
morrow the LORD will shew who are his, and who is holy; and will
cause him to come near unto him: even him whom he hath chosen
will he cause to come near unto him.

Numbers 18:16
And those that are to be redeemed from a month old shalt thou
redeem, according to thine estimation, for the money of five shekels,
after the shekel of the sanctuary, which is twenty gerahs.

Numbers 18:24
But the tithes of the children of Israel, which they offer as an heave
offering unto the LORD, I have given to the Levites to inherit:
therefore I have said unto them, Among the children of Israel they
shall have no inheritance.

Numbers 24:11
Therefore now flee thou to thy place: I thought to promote thee unto
great honour; but, lo, the LORD hath kept thee back from honour.

Numbers 24:20
And when he looked on Amalek, he took up his parable, and said,
Amalek was the first of the nations; but his latter end shall be that he
perish for ever.

Numbers 26:3
And Moses and Eleazar the priest spake with them in the plains of
Moab by Jordan near Jericho, saying,

Numbers 26:63
These are they that were numbered by Moses and Eleazar the priest,
who numbered the children of Israel in the plains of Moab by Jordan
near Jericho.

Numbers 28:2
Command the children of Israel, and say unto them, My offering,
and my bread for my sacrifices made by fire, for a sweet savour unto
me, shall ye observe to offer unto me in their due season.

Numbers 33:50
And the LORD spake unto Moses in the plains of Moab by Jordan
near Jericho, saying,

Numbers 34:15
The two tribes and the half tribe have received their inheritance on
this side Jordan near Jericho eastward, toward the sunrising.

Numbers 35:25
And the congregation shall deliver the slayer out of the hand of the
revenger of blood, and the congregation shall restore him to the city
of his refuge, whither he was fled: and he shall abide in it unto the
death of the high priest, which was anointed with the holy oil.

Deuteronomy 3:19
But your wives, and your little ones, and your cattle, (for I know that
ye have much cattle,) shall abide in your cities which I have given you;

Deuteronomy 6:3
Hear therefore, O Israel, and observe to do it; that it may be well with
thee, and that ye may increase mightily, as the LORD God of thy
fathers hath promised thee, in the land that floweth with milk and
honey.

Deuteronomy 6:5
And thou shalt love the LORD thy God with all thine heart, and
with all thy soul, and with all thy might.

Deuteronomy 7:6
For thou art an holy people unto the LORD thy God: the LORD thy God hath chosen thee to be a special people unto himself, above all people that are upon the face of the earth.

Deuteronomy 8:13
And when thy herds and thy flocks multiply, and thy silver and thy gold is multiplied, and all that thou hast is multiplied;

Deuteronomy 9:5
Not for thy righteousness, or for the uprightness of thine heart, dost thou go to possess their land: but for the wickedness of these nations the LORD thy God doth drive them out from before thee, and that he may perform the word which the LORD sware unto thy fathers, Abraham, Isaac, and Jacob.

Deuteronomy 11:17
And then the LORD's wrath be kindled against you, and he shut up the heaven, that there be no rain, and that the land yield not her fruit; and lest ye perish quickly from off the good land which the LORD giveth you.

Deuteronomy 12:6
And thither ye shall bring your burnt offerings, and your sacrifices, and your tithes, and heave offerings of your hand, and your vows, and your freewill offerings, and the firstlings of your herds and of your flocks:

Deuteronomy 12:21
If the place which the LORD thy God hath chosen to put his name there be too far from thee, then thou shalt kill of thy herd and of thy flock, which the LORD hath given thee, as I have commanded thee, and thou shalt eat in thy gates whatsoever thy soul lusteth after.

Deuteronomy 14:28
At the end of three years thou shalt bring forth all the tithe of thine increase the same year, and shalt lay it up within thy gates:

Deuteronomy 17:17
Neither shall he multiply wives to himself, that his heart turn not away: neither shall he greatly multiply to himself silver and gold.

Deuteronomy 23:25
When thou comest into the standing corn of thy neighbour, then thou mayest pluck the ears with thine hand; but thou shalt not move a sickle unto thy neighbour's standing corn.

Deuteronomy 26:12
When thou hast made an end of tithing all the tithes of thine increase the third year, which is the year of tithing, and hast given it unto the Levite, the stranger, the fatherless, and the widow, that they may eat within thy gates, and be filled;

Deuteronomy 28:50
A nation of fierce countenance, which shall not regard the person of the old, nor shew favour to the young:

Deuteronomy 30:16
In that I command thee this day to love the LORD thy God, to walk in his ways, and to keep his commandments and his statutes and his judgments, that thou mayest live and multiply: and the LORD thy God shall bless thee in the land whither thou goest to possess it.

Deuteronomy 32:46
And he said unto them, Set your hearts unto all the words which I testify among you this day, which ye shall command your children to observe to do, all the words of this law.

Deuteronomy 33:23
And of Naphtali he said, O Naphtali, satisfied with favour, and full with the blessing of the LORD: possess thou the west and the south

Deuteronomy 33:29
Happy art thou, O Israel: who is like unto thee, O people saved by the LORD, the shield of thy help, and who is the sword of thy

excellency! and thine enemies shall be found liars unto thee; and thou shalt tread upon their high places.

Joshua 9:3
And when the inhabitants of Gibeon heard what Joshua had done unto Jericho and to Ai,

Joshua 11:20
For it was of the LORD to harden their hearts, that they should come against Israel in battle, that he might destroy them utterly, and that they might have no favour, but that he might destroy them, as the LORD commanded Moses.

Joshua 13:32
These are the countries which Moses did distribute for inheritance in the plains of Moab, on the other side Jordan, by Jericho, eastward.

Joshua 18:21
Now the cities of the tribe of the children of Benjamin according to their families were Jericho, and Bethhoglah, and the valley of Keziz,

Joshua 24:22
And Joshua said unto the people, Ye are witnesses against yourselves that ye have chosen you the LORD, to serve him. And they said, We are witnesses.

Judges 8:35
Neither shewed they kindness to the house of Jerubbaal, namely, Gideon, according to all the goodness which he had shewed unto Israel.

Ruth 2:20
And Naomi said unto her daughter in law, Blessed be he of the LORD, who hath not left off his kindness to the living and to the dead. And Naomi said unto her, The man is near of kin unto us, one of our next kinsmen.

Ruth 4:4
And I thought to advertise thee, saying, Buy it before the inhabitants, and before the elders of my people. If thou wilt redeem it, redeem it: but if thou wilt not redeem it, then tell me, that I may know: for there is none to redeem it beside thee; and I am after thee. And he said, I will redeem it.

Ruth 4:6
And the kinsman said, I cannot redeem it for myself, lest I mar mine own inheritance: redeem thou my right to thyself; for I cannot redeem it.

Ruth 4:7
Now this was the manner in former time in Israel concerning redeeming and concerning changing, for to confirm all things; a man plucked off his shoe, and gave it to his neighbour: and this was a testimony in Israel.

1 Samuel 12:13
Now therefore behold the king whom ye have chosen, and whom ye have desired! and, behold, the LORD hath set a king over you.

1 Samuel 15:28
And Samuel said unto him, The LORD hath rent the kingdom of Israel from thee this day, and hath given it to a neighbour of thine, that is better than thou.

1 Samuel 16:22
And Saul sent to Jesse, saying, Let David, I pray thee, stand before me; for he hath found favour in my sight.

1 Samuel 22:23
Abide thou with me, fear not: for he that seeketh my life seeketh thy life: but with me thou shalt be in safeguard.

2 Samuel 3:8
Then was Abner very wroth for the words of Ishbosheth, and said, Am I a dog's head, which against Judah do shew kindness this day unto the house of Saul thy father, to his brethren, and to his friends, and have not delivered thee into the hand of David, that thou chargest me to day with a fault concerning this woman?

2 Samuel 7:23
And what one nation in the earth is like thy people, even like Israel, whom God went to redeem for a people to himself, and to make him a name, and to do for you great things and terrible, for thy land, before thy people, which thou redeemedst to thee from Egypt, from the nations and their gods?

2 Samuel 19:9
And all the people were at strife throughout all the tribes of Israel, saying, The king saved us out of the hand of our enemies, and he delivered us out of the hand of the Philistines; and now he is fled out of the land for Absalom.

2 Samuel 21:2
And the king called the Gibeonites, and said unto them; (now the Gibeonites were not of the children of Israel, but of the remnant of the Amorites; and the children of Israel had sworn unto them: and Saul sought to slay them in his zeal to the children of Israel and Judah.)

2 Samuel 22:4
I will call on the LORD, who is worthy to be praised: so shall I be saved from mine enemies.

2 Samuel 23:10
He arose, and smote the Philistines until his hand was weary, and his hand clave unto the sword: and the LORD wrought a great victory that day; and the people returned after him only to spoil.

1 Kings 1:40
And all the people came up after him, and the people piped with pipes, and rejoiced with great joy, so that the earth rent with the sound of them.

1 Kings 3:5
In Gibeon the LORD appeared to Solomon in a dream by night: and God said, Ask what I shall give thee.

1Kings 3:6
And Solomon said, Thou hast shewed unto thy servant David my father great mercy, according as he walked before thee in truth, and in righteousness, and in uprightness of heart with thee; and thou hast kept for him this great kindness, that thou hast given him a son to sit on his throne, as it is this day;

1 Kings 9:4
And if thou wilt walk before me, as David thy father walked, in integrity of heart, and in uprightness, to do according to all that I have commanded thee, and wilt keep my statutes and my judgments:

1 Kings 10:1
And when the queen of Sheba heard of the fame of Solomon concerning the name of the LORD, she came to prove him with hard questions.

1 Kings 10:4
And when the queen of Sheba had seen all Solomon's wisdom, and the house that he had built,

1 Kings 10:10
And she gave the king an hundred and twenty talents of gold, and of spices very great store, and precious stones: there came no more such abundance of spices as these which the queen of Sheba gave to king Solomon.

1 Kings 10:13
And king Solomon gave unto the queen of Sheba all her desire, whatsoever she asked, beside that which Solomon gave her of his royal bounty. So she turned and went to her own country, she and her servants.

1 Kings 11:19
And Hadad found great favour in the sight of Pharaoh, so that he gave him to wife the sister of his own wife, the sister of Tahpenes the queen.

1 Kings 15:13
And also Maachah his mother, even her he removed from being queen, because she had made an idol in a grove; and Asa destroyed her idol, and burnt it by the brook Kidron.

1 Kings 16:34
In his days did Hiel the Bethelite build Jericho: he laid the foundation thereof in Abiram his firstborn, and set up the gates thereof in his youngest son Segub, according to the word of the LORD, which he spake by Joshua the son of Nun.

1 Kings 20:35
And a certain man of the sons of the prophets said unto his neighbour in the word of the LORD, Smite me, I pray thee. And the man refused to smite him.

2 Kings 10:13
Jehu met with the brethren of Ahaziah king of Judah, and said, Who are ye? And they answered, We are the brethren of Ahaziah; and we go down to salute the children of the king and the children of the queen.

2 Kings 10:16
And he said, Come with me, and see my zeal for the LORD. So they made him ride in his chariot.

1 Chronicles 16:25
For great is the LORD, and greatly to be praised: he also is to be feared above all gods.

1 Chronicles 16:29
Give unto the LORD the glory due unto his name: bring an offering, and come before him: worship the LORD in the beauty of holiness.

1 Chronicles 28:9
And thou, Solomon my son, know thou the God of thy father, and serve him with a perfect heart and with a willing mind: for the LORD searcheth all hearts, and understandeth all the imaginations of the thoughts: if thou seek him, he will be found of thee; but if thou forsake him, he will cast thee off for ever.

1 Chronicles 28:21
And, behold, the courses of the priests and the Levites, even they shall be with thee for all the service of the house of God: and there shall be with thee for all manner of workmanship every willing skilful man, for any manner of service: also the princes and all the people will be wholly at thy commandment.

1 Chronicles 29:1
Furthermore David the king said unto all the congregation, Solomon my son, whom alone God hath chosen, is yet young and tender, and the work is great: for the palace is not for man, but for the LORD God.

1 Chronicles 29:11
Thine, O LORD, is the greatness, and the power, and the glory, and the victory, and the majesty: for all that is in the heaven and in the earth is thine; thine is the kingdom, O LORD, and thou art exalted as head above all.

1 Chronicles 29:17
I know also, my God, that thou triest the heart, and hast pleasure
in uprightness. As for me, in the uprightness of mine heart I have
willingly offered all these things: and now have I seen with joy thy
people, which are present here, to offer willingly unto thee.

2 Chronicles 6:6
But I have chosen Jerusalem, that my name might be there; and have
chosen David to be over my people Israel.

2 Chronicles 9:1
And when the queen of Sheba heard of the fame of Solomon, she
came to prove Solomon with hard questions at Jerusalem, with a very
great company, and camels that bare spices, and gold in abundance,
and precious stones: and when she was come to Solomon, she
communed with him of all that was in her heart.

2 Chronicles 9:9
And she gave the king an hundred and twenty talents of gold, and
of spices great abundance, and precious stones: neither was there any
such spice as the queen of Sheba gave king Solomon.

2 Chronicles 15:16
And also concerning Maachah the mother of Asa the king, he removed
her from being queen, because she had made an idol in a grove: and Asa
cut down her idol, and stamped it, and burnt it at the brook Kidron.

2 Chronicles 20:21
And when he had consulted with the people, he appointed singers
unto the LORD, and that should praise the beauty of holiness, as
they went out before the army, and to say, Praise the LORD; for his
mercy endureth for ever.

2 Chronicles 31:18
And to the genealogy of all their little ones, their wives, and their
sons, and their daughters, through all the congregation: for in their
set office they sanctified themselves in holiness:

2 Chronicles 32:10
Thus saith Sennacherib king of Assyria, Whereon do ye trust, that ye abide in the siege in Jerusalem?

Nehemiah 1:5
And said, I beseech thee, O LORD God of heaven, the great and terrible God, that keepeth covenant and mercy for them that love him and observe his commandments:

Nehemiah 2:6
And the king said unto me, (the queen also sitting by him,) For how long shall thy journey be? and when wilt thou return? So it pleased the king to send me; and I set him a time.

Nehemiah 3:2
And next unto him builded the men of Jericho. And next to them builded Zaccur the son of Imri.

Nehemiah 5:5
Yet now our flesh is as the flesh of our brethren, our children as their children: and, lo, we bring into bondage our sons and our daughters to be servants, and some of our daughters are brought unto bondage already: neither is it in our power to redeem them; for other men have our lands and vineyards.

Nehemiah 8:17
And all the congregation of them that were come again out of the captivity made booths, and sat under the booths: for since the days of Jeshua the son of Nun unto that day had not the children of Israel done so. And there was very great gladness.

Nehemiah 9:17
And refused to obey, neither were mindful of thy wonders that thou didst among them; but hardened their necks, and in their rebellion appointed a captain to return to their bondage: but thou art a God ready to pardon, gracious and merciful, slow to anger, and of great kindness, and forsookest them not.

Nehemiah 10:38
And the priest the son of Aaron shall be with the Levites, when the Levites take tithes: and the Levites shall bring up the tithe of the tithes unto the house of our God, to the chambers, into the treasure house.

Nehemiah 12:44
And at that time were some appointed over the chambers for the treasures, for the offerings, for the firstfruits, and for the tithes, to gather into them out of the fields of the cities the portions of the law for the priests and Levites: for Judah rejoiced for the priests and for the Levites that waited.

Esther 1:4
When he showed the riches of his glorious kingdom and the hounur of his excellent majesty many days ever an hundred and fourscore days.

Esther 1:11
To bring Vashti the queen before the king with the crown royal, to shew the people and the princes her beauty: for she was fair to look on.

Esther 2:9
And the maiden pleased him, and she obtained kindness of him; and he speedily gave her her things for purification, with such things as belonged to her, and seven maidens, which were meet to be given her, out of the king's house: and he preferred her and her maids unto the best place of the house of the women.

Esther 2:17
And the king loved Esther above all the women, and she obtained grace and favour in his sight more than all the virgins; so that he set the royal crown upon her head, and made her queen instead of Vashti.

Esther 4:4
So Esther's maids and her chamberlains came and told it her. Then was the queen exceedingly grieved; and she sent raiment to clothe Mordecai, and to take away his sackcloth from him: but he received it not.

Esther 8:5
And said, If it please the king, and if I have found favour in his sight, and the thing seem right before the king, and I be pleasing in his eyes, let it be written to reverse the letters devised by Haman the son of Hammedatha the Agagite, which he wrote to destroy the Jews which are in all the king's provinces:

Esther 8:6
For how can I endure to see the evil that shall come unto my people? or how can I endure to see the destruction of my kindred?

Job 4:6
Is not this thy fear, thy confidence, thy hope, and the uprightness of thy ways?

Job 6:23
Or, Deliver me from the enemy's hand? or, Redeem me from the hand of the mighty?

Job 8:7
Though thy beginning was small, yet thy latter end should greatly increase.

Job 8:15
He shall lean upon his house, but it shall not stand: he shall hold it fast, but it shall not endure.

Job 10:12
Thou hast granted me life and favour, and thy visitation hath preserved my spirit.

Job 12:4
I am as one mocked of his neighbour, who calleth upon God, and he answereth him: the just upright man is laughed to scorn.

Job 29:1
Moreover Job continued his parable, and said,

Job 29:18
Then I said, I shall die in my nest, and I shall multiply my days as the sand.

Job 33:3
My words shall be of the uprightness of my heart: and my lips shall utter knowledge clearly.

Job 33:15
In a dream, in a vision of the night, when deep sleep falleth upon men, in slumberings upon the bed;

Job 37:23
Touching the Almighty we cannot find him out: he is excellent in power, and in judgment, and in plenty of justice he will not afflict.

Job 39:9
Will the unicorn be willing to serve thee, or abide by thy crib?

Psalms 8:1
O Lord our Lord how excellent is thy name in all the earth who hast set thy glory above the heavens.

Psalms 9:7
But the LORD shall endure for ever: he hath prepared his throne for judgment.

Psalms 9:8
And he shall judge the world in righteousness, he shall minister judgment to the people in uprightness.

Psalms 12:2
They speak vanity every one with his neighbour: with flattering lips and with a double heart do they speak.

Psalms 21:5
His glory is great in thy salvation: honour and majesty hast thou laid upon him.

Psalms 25:21
Let integrity and uprightness preserve me; for I wait on thee.

Psalms 26:11
But as for me, I will walk in mine integrity: redeem me, and be merciful unto me.

Psalms 29:2
Give unto the LORD the glory due unto his name; worship the LORD in the beauty of holiness.

Psalms 30:5
For his anger endureth but a moment; in his favour is life: weeping may endure for a night, but joy cometh in the morning.

Psalms 31:21
Blessed be the LORD: for he hath shewed me his marvellous kindness in a strong city.

Psalms 36:7
How excellent is thy lovingkindness, O God! therefore the children of men put their trust under the shadow of the wings.

Psalms 40:16
Let all those that seek thee rejoice and be glad in thee: let such as love thy salvation say continually, The LORD be magnified.

Psalms 47:8
God reigneth over the heathen: God sitteth upon the throne of his holiness.

Psalms 48:1
Great is the LORD, and greatly to be praised in the city of our God, in the mountain of his holiness.

Psalms 49:4
I will incline mine ear to a parable: I will open my dark saying upon the harp.

Psalms 49:15
But God will redeem my soul from the power of the grave: for he shall receive me. Selah.

Psalms 60:6
God hath spoken in his holiness; I will rejoice, I will divide Shechem, and mete out the valley of Succoth.

Psalms 67:6
Then shall the earth yield her increase; and God, even our own God, shall bless us.

Psalms 69:9
For the zeal of thine house hath eaten me up; and the reproaches of them that reproached thee are fallen upon me.

Psalms 71:21
Thou shalt increase my greatness, and comfort me on every side.

Psalms 72:5
They shall fear thee as long as the sun and moon endure, throughout all generations.

Psalms 72:14
He shall redeem their soul from deceit and violence: and precious shall their blood be in his sight.

Psalms 72:17
His name shall endure for ever: his name shall be continued as long as the sun: and men shall be blessed in him: all nations shall call him blessed.

Psalms 73:20
As a dream when one awaketh; so, O Lord, when thou awakest, thou shalt despise their image.

Psalms 76:4
Thou art more glorious and excellent, than the mountains of prey.

Psalms 89:3
I have made a covenant with my chosen, I have sworn unto David my servant,

Psalms 93:5
Thy testimonies are very sure: holiness becometh thine house, O LORD, for ever.

Psalms 98:1
O sing unto the LORD a new song; for he hath done marvellous things: his right hand, and his holy arm, hath gotten him the victory.

Psalms 102:12
But thou, O LORD, shalt endure for ever; and thy remembrance unto all generations.

Psalms 102:14
For thy servants take pleasure in her stones, and favour the dust thereof.

Psalms 106:8
Nevertheless he saved them for his name's sake, that he might make his mighty power to be known.

Psalms 107:37
And sow the fields, and plant vineyards, which may yield fruits of increase.

Psalms 107:43
Whoso is wise, and will observe these things, even they shall understand the loving-kindness of the LORD.

Psalms 110:3
Thy people shall be willing in the day of thy power, in the beauties of holiness from the womb of the morning: thou hast the dew of thy youth.

Psalms 111:8
They stand fast for ever and ever, and are done in truth and uprightness.

Psalms 117:2
For his merciful kindness is great toward us: and the truth of the LORD endureth for ever. Praise ye the LORD.

Psalms 119:7
I will praise thee with uprightness of heart, when I shall have learned thy righteous judgments.

Psalms 119:58
I intreated thy favour with my whole heart: be merciful unto me according to thy word.

Psalms 119:139
My zeal hath consumed me, because mine enemies have forgotten thy words.

Psalms 141:5
Let the righteous smite me; it shall be a kindness: and let him reprove me; it shall be an excellent oil, which shall not break my head: for yet my prayer also shall be in their calamities.

Psalms 143:10
Teach me to do thy will; for thou art my God: thy spirit is good; lead me into the land of uprightness.

Psalms 150:2
Praise him for his mighty acts: praise him according to his excellent greatness

Proverbs 1:5
A wise man will hear, and will increase learning; and a man of understanding shall attain unto wise counsels:

Proverbs 7:21
With her much fair speech she caused him to yield, with the flattering of her lips she forced him.

Proverbs 11:9
An hypocrite with his mouth destroyeth his neighbour: but through knowledge shall the just be delivered.

Proverbs 14:2
He that walketh in his uprightness feareth the LORD: but he that is perverse in his ways despiseth him.

Proverbs 14:21
He that despiseth his neighbour sinneth: but he that hath mercy on the poor, happy is he.

Proverbs 19:6
Many will intreat the favour of the prince: and every man is a friend to him that giveth gifts.

Proverbs 23:26
My son, give me thine heart, and let thine eyes observe my ways.

Proverbs 26:7
The legs of the lame are not equal: so is a parable in the mouth of fools.

Proverbs 28:6
Better is the poor that walketh in his uprightness, than he that is perverse in his ways, though he be rich.

Ecclesiastes 5:11
When goods increase, they are increased that eat them: and what good is there to the owners thereof, saving the beholding of them with their eyes?

Isaiah 1:19
If ye be willing and obedient, ye shall eat the good of the land:

Isaiah 3:5
And the people shall be oppressed, every one by another, and every one by his neighbour: the child shall behave himself proudly against the ancient, and the base against the honourable.

Isaiah 5:10
Yea, ten acres of vineyard shall yield one bath, and the seed of an homer shall yield an ephah.

Isaiah 9:7
Of the increase of his government and peace there shall be no end, upon the throne of David, and upon his kingdom, to order it, and to establish it with judgment and with justice from henceforth even for ever. The zeal of the LORD of hosts will perform this.

Isaiah 25:8
He will swallow up death in victory; and the Lord GOD will wipe away tears from off all faces; and the rebuke of his people shall he take away from off all the earth: for the LORD hath spoken it.

Isaiah 26:7
The way of the just is uprightness: thou, most upright, dost weigh the path of the just.

Isaiah 26:10
Let favour be shewed to the wicked, yet will he not learn righteousness: in the land of uprightness will he deal unjustly, and will not behold the majesty of the LORD.

Isaiah 29:7
And the multitude of all the nations that fight against Ariel, even all that fight against her and her munition, and that distress her, shall be as a dream of a night vision.

Isaiah 37:32
For out of Jerusalem shall go forth a remnant, and they that escape out of mount Zion: the zeal of the LORD of hosts shall do this.

Isaiah 41:6
They helped every one his neighbour; and every one said to his brother, Be of good courage.

Isaiah41:8
But thou, Israel, art my servant, Jacob whom I have chosen, the seed of Abraham my friend.

Isaiah 45:17
But Israel shall be saved in the LORD with an everlasting salvation: ye shall not be ashamed nor confounded world without end.

Isaiah 54:8
In a little wrath I hid my face from thee for a moment; but with everlasting kindness will I have mercy on thee, saith the LORD thy Redeemer.

Isaiah 59:17
For he put on righteousness as a breastplate, and an helmet of salvation upon his head; and he put on the garments of vengeance for clothing, and was clad with zeal as a cloak.

Isaiah 60:10
And the sons of strangers shall build up thy walls, and their kings shall minister unto thee: for in my wrath I smote thee, but in my favour have I had mercy on thee.

Isaiah 63:15
Look down from heaven, and behold from the habitation of thy holiness and of thy glory: where is thy zeal and thy strength, the sounding of thy bowels and of thy mercies toward me? are they restrained?

Isaiah 63:18
The people of thy holiness have possessed it but a little while: our adversaries have trodden down thy sanctuary.

Jeremiah 2:2
Go and cry in the ears of Jerusalem, saying, Thus saith the LORD; I remember thee, the kindness of thy youth, the love of thine espousals, when thou wentest after me in the wilderness, in a land that was not sown.

Jeremiah 2:3
Israel was holiness unto the LORD, and the firstfruits of his increase: all that devour him shall offend; evil shall come upon them, saith the LORD.

Jeremiah 10:10
But the LORD is the true God, he is the living God, and an
everlasting king: at his wrath the earth shall tremble, and the nations
shall not be able to abide his indignation.

Jeremiah 13:18
Say unto the king and to the queen, Humble yourselves, sit down: for
your principalities shall come down, even the crown of your glory.

Jeremiah 16:13
Therefore will I cast you out of this land into a land that ye know not,
neither ye nor your fathers; and there shall ye serve other gods day
and night; where I will not shew you favour.

Jeremiah 23:6
In his days Judah shall be saved, and Israel shall dwell safely: and
this is his name whereby he shall be called, THE LORD OUR
RIGHTEOUSNESS.

Jeremiah 23:28
The prophet that hath a dream, let him tell a dream; and he that hath
my word, let him speak my word faithfully. What is the chaff to the
wheat? saith the LORD.

Jeremiah 30:19
And out of them shall proceed thanksgiving and the voice of them
that make merry: and I will multiply them, and they shall not be few;
I will also glorify them, and they shall not be small.

Jeremiah 31:3
The LORD hath appeared of old unto me, saying, Yea, I have loved
thee with an everlasting love: therefore with loving-kindness have I
drawn thee.

Jeremiah 31:23
Thus saith the LORD of hosts, the God of Israel; As yet they shall use
this speech in the land of Judah and in the cities thereof, when I shall

bring again their captivity; The LORD bless thee, O habitation of justice, and mountain of holiness.

Jeremiah 31: 34
And they shall teach no more every man his neighbour, and every man his brother, saying, Know the LORD: for they shall all know me, from the least of them unto the greatest of them, saith the LORD: for I will forgive their iniquity, and I will remember their sin no more.

Jeremiah 33:22
As the host of heaven cannot be numbered, neither the sand of the sea measured: so will I multiply the seed of David my servant, and the Levites that minister unto me.

Jeremiah 52:8
But the army of the Chaldeans pursued after the king, and overtook Zedekiah in the plains of Jericho; and all his army was scattered from him.

Ezekiel 5:13
Thus shall mine anger be accomplished, and I will cause my fury to rest upon them, and I will be comforted: and they shall know that I the LORD have spoken it in my zeal, when I have accomplished my fury in them.

Ezekiel 17: 2
Son of man, put forth a riddle, and speak a parable unto the house of Israel;

Ezekiel 22:14
Can thine heart endure, or can thine hands be strong, in the days that I shall deal with thee? I the LORD have spoken it, and will do it.

Ezekiel 34:27
And the tree of the field shall yield her fruit, and the earth shall yield her increase, and they shall be safe in their land, and shall know that

I am the LORD, when I have broken the bands of their yoke, and delivered them out of the hand of those that served themselves of them.

Ezekiel 36:11
And I will multiply upon you man and beast; and they shall increase and bring fruit: and I will settle you after your old estates, and will do better unto you than at your beginnings: and ye shall know that I am the LORD.

Ezekiel 36:30
And I will multiply the fruit of the tree, and the increase of the field, that ye shall receive no more reproach of famine among the heathen.

Daniel 1:9
Now God had brought Daniel into favour and tender love with the prince of the eunuchs.

Daniel 2:6
But if ye shew the dream, and the interpretation thereof, ye shall receive of me gifts and rewards and great honour: therefore shew me the dream, and the interpretation thereof.

Daniel 2:31
Thou, O king savest, and behold a great image this great image, whose brightness was excellent, stood before thee: and the form thereof was terrible.

Daniel 4:36
At the same time my reason returned unto me;. And for the glory of my kindness, mine honour and brightness returned unto me; and my counsellors and my lords sought unto me and I was established in my kingdom and excellent majesty was added unto me.

Daniel 5:10
Now the queen by reason of the words of the king and his lords came into the banquet house: and the queen spake and said, O king, live

for ever: let not thy thoughts trouble thee, nor let thy countenance be changed:

Hosea 8:7
For they have sown the wind, and they shall reap the whirlwind: it hath no stalk: the bud shall yield no meal: if so be it yield, the strangers shall swallow it up.

Hosea 13:14
I will ransom them from the power of the grave; I will redeem them from death: O death, I will be thy plagues; O grave, I will be thy destruction: repentance shall be hid from mine eyes.

Joel 2:13
And rend your heart, and not your garments, and turn unto the LORD your God: for he is gracious and merciful, slow to anger, and of great kindness, and repenteth him of the evil.

Joel 2:22
Be not afraid, ye beasts of the field: for the pastures of the wilderness do spring, for the tree beareth her fruit, the fig tree and the vine do yield their strength.

Amos 4:2
The Lord GOD hath sworn by his holiness, that, lo, the days shall come upon you, that he will take you away with hooks, and your posterity with fishhooks.

Amos 4:4
Come to Bethel, and transgress; at Gilgal multiply transgression; and bring your sacrifices every morning, and your tithes after three years:

Jonah 4:2
And he prayed unto the LORD, and said, I pray thee, O LORD, was not this my saying, when I was yet in my country? Therefore I fled before unto Tarshish: for I knew that thou art a gracious God, and merciful, slow to anger, and of great kindness, and repentest thee of the evil.

Habakkuk 2:6
Shall not all these take up a parable against him, and a taunting proverb against him, and say, Woe to him that increaseth that which is not his! how long? and to him that ladeth himself with thick clay!

Malachi 3:8
Will a man rob God? Yet ye have robbed me. But ye say, Wherein have we robbed thee? In tithes and offerings.

Malachi 3:10
Bring ye all the tithes into the storehouse, that there may be meat in mine house, and prove me now herewith, saith the LORD of hosts, if I will not open you the windows of heaven, and pour you out a blessing, that there shall not be room enough to receive it.

Matthew 1:19
Then Joseph her husband, being a just man, and not willing to make her a publick example, was minded to put her away privily.

Matthew 2:12
And being warned of God in a dream that they should not return to Herod, they departed into their own country another way.

Matthew 3:16
And Jesus, when he was baptized, went up straightway out of the water: and, lo, the heavens were opened unto him, and he saw the Spirit of God descending like a dove, and lighting upon him:

Matthew 5:12
Rejoice, and be exceeding glad: for great is your reward in heaven: for so persecuted they the prophets which were before you.

Matthew 10:11
And into whatsoever city or town ye shall enter, enquire who in it is worthy; and there abide till ye go thence.

Matthew 12:20
A bruised reed shall he not break, and smoking flax shall he not quench, till he send forth judgment unto victory.

Matthew 13:24
Another parable put he forth unto them, saying, The kingdom of heaven is likened unto a man which sowed good seed in his field:

Matthew 13:34
All these things spake Jesus unto the multitude in parables; and without a parable spake he not unto them:

Matthew 15:28
Then Jesus answered and said unto her, O woman, great is thy faith: be it unto thee even as thou wilt. And her daughter was made whole from that very hour.

Matthew 19:19
Honour thy father and thy mother: and, Thou shalt love thy neighbour as thyself.

Matthew 19:25
When his disciples heard it, they were exceedingly amazed, saying, Who then can be saved?

Matthew 20:22
But Jesus answered and said, Ye know not what ye ask. Are ye able to drink of the cup that I shall drink of, and to be baptized with the baptism that I am baptized with? They say unto him, We are able.

Matthew 20:26
But it shall not be so among you: but whosoever will be great among you, let him be your minister;

Matthew 20:29
And as they departed from Jericho, a great multitude followed him.

Matthew 22:36
Master, which is the great commandment in the law?

Matthew 24:13
But he that shall endure unto the end, the same shall be saved.

Matthew 28:20
Teaching them to observe all things whatsoever I have commanded you: and, lo, I am with you alway, even unto the end of the world. Amen.

Mark 1:8
I indeed have baptized you with water: but he shall baptize you with the Holy Ghost.

Mark 4:8
And other fell on good ground, and did yield fruit that sprang up and increased; and brought forth, some thirty, and some sixty, and some an hundred.

Mark 4:34
But without a parable spake he not unto them: and when they were alone, he expounded all things to his disciples.

Mark 6:10
And he said unto them, In what place soever ye enter into an house, there abide till ye depart from that place.

Mark 10:26
And they were astonished out of measure, saying among themselves, Who then can be saved?

Mark 10:46
And they came to Jericho: and as he went out of Jericho with his disciples and a great number of people, blind Bartimaeus, the son of Timaeus, sat by the highway side begging.

Mark 12:12
And they sought to lay hold on him, but feared the people: for they knew that he had spoken the parable against them: and they left him, and went their way.

Mark 12:31
And the second is like, namely this, Thou shalt love thy neighbour as thyself. There is none other commandment greater than these.

Mark 12:33
And to love him with all the heart, and with all the understanding, and with all the soul, and with all the strength, and to love his neighbour as himself, is more than all whole burnt offerings and sacrifices.

Mark 13:13
And ye shall be hated of all men for my name's sake: but he that shall endure unto the end, the same shall be saved.

Mark 13:20
And except that the Lord had shortened those days, no flesh should be saved: but for the elect's sake, whom he hath chosen, he hath shortened the days.

Mark 15:15
And so Pilate, willing to content the people, released Barabbas unto them, and delivered Jesus, when he had scourged him, to be crucified.

Mark 16:16
He that believeth and is baptized shall be saved; but he that believeth not shall be damned.

Luke 1:30
And the angel said unto her, Fear not, Mary: for thou hast found favour with God.

Luke1:75
In holiness and righteousness before him, all the days of our life.

Luke 3:21
Now when all the people were baptized, it came to pass, that Jesus also being baptized, and praying, the heaven was opened,

Luke 7:29
And all the people that heard him, and the publicans, justified God, being baptized with the baptism of John.

Luke 10:2
Therefore said he unto them, The harvest truly is great, but the labourers are few: pray ye therefore the Lord of the harvest, that he would send forth labourers into his harvest.

Luke 10:27
And he answering said, Thou shalt love the Lord thy God with all thy heart, and with all thy soul, and with all thy strength, and with all thy mind; and thy neighbour as thyself.

Luke 10:29
But he, willing to justify himself, said unto Jesus, And who is my neighbour?

Luke 12:16
And he spake a parable unto them, saying, The ground of a certain rich man brought forth plentifully:

Luke 12:50
But I have a baptism to be baptized with; and how am I straitened till it be accomplished!

Luke 18:12
I fast twice in the week, I give tithes of all that I possess.

Luke 19:1
And Jesus entered and passed through Jericho.

Luke 19:5
And when Jesus came to the place, he looked up, and saw him, and said unto him, Zacchaeus, make haste, and come down; for to day I must abide at thy house.

Luke 19:11
And as they heard these things, he added and spake a parable, because he was nigh to Jerusalem, and because they thought that the kingdom of God should immediately appear.

Luke 23:35
And the people stood beholding and the rulers also with them derided him, saying, He saved others; let him save himself, if he be Christ, the chosen of God.

John 2:17
And his disciples remembered that it was written, The zeal of thine house hath eaten me up.

John 3:17
For God sent not his Son into the world to condemn the world; but that the world through him might be saved.

John 3:22
After these things came Jesus and his disciples into the land of Judaea; and there he tarried with them, and baptized.

John 3:30
He must increase, but I must decrease.

John 5:35
He was a burning and a shining light: and ye were willing for a season to rejoice in his light.

John 13:18
I speak not of you all: I know whom I have chosen: but that the scripture may be fulfilled, He that eateth bread with me hath lifted up his heel against me.

John 14:16
And I will pray the Father, and he shall give you another Comforter, that he may abide with you for ever;

John 15:13
Greater love hath no man than this, that a man lay down his life for his friends.

Acts 1:2
Until the day in which he was taken up, after that he through the Holy Ghost had given commandments unto the apostles whom he had chosen:

Acts 2:17
And it shall come to pass in the last days, saith God, I will pour out of my Spirit upon all flesh: and your sons and your daughters shall prophesy, and your young men shall see visions, and your old men shall dream dreams:

Acts 2:38
Then Peter said unto them, Repent, and be baptized every one of you in the name of Jesus Christ for the remission of sins, and ye shall receive the gift of the Holy Ghost.

Acts 2:41
Then they that gladly received his word were baptized: and the same day there were added unto them about three thousand souls.

Acts 4:12
Neither is there salvation in any other: for there is none other name under heaven given among men, whereby we must be saved.

Acts 7:46
Who found favour before God, and desire to find a tabernacle for the God of Jacob.

Acts 8:12
But when they believed Philip preaching the things concerning the kingdom of God, and the name of Jesus Christ, they were baptized, both men and women.

Acts 8:38
And he commanded the chariot to stand still: and they went down both into the water, both Philip and the eunuch; and he baptized him.

Acts 16:15
And when she was baptized, and her household, she besought us, saying, If ye have judged me to be faithful to the Lord, come into my house, and abide there. And she constrained us.

Acts 21:25
As touching the Gentiles which believe, we have written and concluded that they observe no such thing, save only that they keep themselves from things offered to idols, and from blood, and from strangled, and from fornication.

Acts 23:21
But do not thou yield unto them: for there lie in wait for him of them more than forty men, which have bound themselves with an oath, that they will neither eat nor drink till they have killed him: and now are they ready, looking for a promise from thee.

Acts 27:43
But the centurion, willing to save Paul, kept them from their purpose; and commanded that they which could swim should cast themselves first into the sea, and get to land:

Romans 6:13
Neither yield ye your members as instruments of unrighteousness unto sin: but yield yourselves unto God, as those that are alive from the dead, and your members as instruments of righteousness unto God.

Romans 6:16
Know ye not, that to whom ye yield yourselves servants to obey, his servants ye are to whom ye obey; whether of sin unto death, or of obedience unto righteousness?

Romans 6:22
But now being made free from sin, and become servants to God, ye have your fruit unto holiness, and the end everlasting life.

Romans 8:24
For we are saved by hope: but hope that is seen is not hope: for what a man seeth, why doth he yet hope for?

Romans 8:28
And we know that all things work together for good to them that love God, to them who are the called according to his purpose.

Romans 9:22
What if God, willing to shew his wrath, and to make his power known, endured with much longsuffering the vessels of wrath fitted to destruction:

Romans 10:1
Brethren, my heart's desire and prayer to God for Israel is, that they might be saved.

Romans 10:2
For I bear them record that they have a zeal of God, but not according to knowledge.

Romans 13:10
Love worketh no ill to his neighbour: therefore love is the fulfilling of
the law.

1 Corinthians 3:6
I have planted, Apollos watered; but God gave the increase.

1 Corinthians 3:15
If any man's work shall be burned, he shall suffer loss: but he himself
shall be saved; yet so as by fire.

1 Corinthians 12:13
For by one Spirit are we all baptized into one body, whether we be
Jews or Gentiles, whether we be bond or free; and have been all made
to drink into one Spirit.

1 Corinthians 15:57
But thanks be to God, which giveth us the victory through our Lord
Jesus Christ.

2 Corinthians 2:15
For we are unto God a sweet savour of Christ, in them that are saved,
and in them that perish:

2 Corinthians 5:8
We are confident, I say, and willing rather to be absent from the body,
and to be present with the Lord.

2 Corinthians 6:6
By pureness, by knowledge, by longsuffering, by kindness, by the
Holy Ghost, by love unfeigned,

2 Corinthians 7:1
Having therefore these promises, dearly beloved, let us cleanse
ourselves from all filthiness of the flesh and spirit, perfecting holiness
in the fear of God.

2 Corinthians 7:11
For behold this selfsame thing, that ye sorrowed after a godly sort, what carefulness it wrought in you, yea, what clearing of yourselves, yea, what indignation, yea, what fear, yea, what vehement desire, yea, what zeal, yea, what revenge! In all things ye have approved yourselves to be clear in this matter.

2 Corinthians 9:2
For I know the forwardness of your mind, for which I boast of you to them of Macedonia, that Achaia was ready a year ago; and your zeal hath provoked very many.

2 Corinthians 9:10
Now he that ministereth seed to the sower both minister bread for your food, and multiply your seed sown, and increase the fruits of your righteousness;)

Galatians 4:5
To redeem them that were under the law, that we might receive the adoption of sons.

Galatians 5:22
But the fruit of the Spirit is love, joy, peace, longsuffering, gentleness, goodness, faith,

Ephesians 2:8
For by grace are ye saved through faith; and that not of yourselves: it is the gift of God:

Ephesians 6:24
Grace be with all them that love our Lord Jesus Christ in sincerity. Amen.

Philippians 1:9
And this I pray, that your love may abound yet more and more in knowledge and in all judgment.

Philippians 1:10
That ye may approve things that are excellent: that ye maybe sincere and without offence till the day of Christ:

Philippians 3:6
Concerning zeal, persecuting the church; touching the righteousness which is in the law, blameless.

Colossians 3:12
Put on therefore, as the elect of God, holy and beloved, bowels of mercies, kindness, humbleness of mind, meekness, longsuffering;

1 Thessalonians 3:12
And the Lord make you to increase and abound in love one toward another, and toward all men, even as we do toward you:

1 Thessalonians 5:8
But let us, who are of the day, be sober, putting on the breastplate of faith and love; and for an helmet, the hope of salvation.

2 Thessalonians 1:4
So that we ourselves glory in you in the churches of God for your patience and faith in all your persecutions and tribulations that ye endure:

2 Thessalonians 2:13
But we are bound to give thanks alway to God for you, brethren beloved of the Lord, because God hath from the beginning chosen you to salvation through sanctification of the Spirit and belief of the truth:

1 Timothy 2:4
Who will have all men to be saved, and to come unto the knowledge of the truth.

1 Timothy 3:16
And without controversy great is the mystery of godliness: God was manifest in the flesh, justified in the Spirit, seen of angels, preached unto the Gentiles, believed on in the world, received up into glory.

1 Timothy 6:18
That they do good, that they be rich in good works, ready to distribute, willing to communicate;

II Timothy 4:5
But watch thou in all things, endure afflictions, do the work of an evangelist, make full proof of thy ministry.

2 Timothy 4:8
Henceforth there is laid up for me a crown of righteousness, which the Lord, the righteous judge, shall give me at that day: and not to me only, but unto all them also that love his appearing.

Titus 2:14
Who gave himself for us, that he might redeem us from all iniquity, and purify unto himself a peculiar people, zealous of good works.

Titus 3:4
But after that the kindness and love of God our Saviour toward man appeared,

Hebrews 1:4
Being made so much better than the angels as he hath by inheritance obtained a more excellent name that they.

Hebrews 2:3
How shall we escape, if we neglect so great salvation; which at the first began to be spoken by the Lord, and was confirmed unto us by them that heard him;

Hebrews 6:14
Saying, Surely blessing I will bless thee, and multiplying I will multiply thee.

Hebrews 6:17
Wherein God, willing more abundantly to shew unto the heirs of promise the immutability of his counsel, confirmed it by an oath:

Hebrews 7:5
And verily they that are of the sons of Levi, who receive the office of the priesthood, have a commandment to take tithes of the people according to the law, that is, of their brethren, though they come out of the loins of Abraham:

Hebrews 7:6
But he whose descent is not counted from them received tithes of Abraham, and blessed him that had the promises.

Hebrews 7:8
And here men that die receive tithes; but there he receiveth them, of whom it is witnessed that he liveth.

Hebrews 8:6
But now hath he obtained a more excellent ministry, by how much also he is the mediator of a better covenant which was established upon better promises.

Hebrews 11:30
By faith the walls of Jericho fell down, after they were compassed about seven days.

Hebrews 12:1
Wherefore seeing we also are compassed about with so great a cloud of witnesses, let us lay aside every weight, and the sin which doth so easily beset us, and let us run with patience the race that is set before us,

Hebrews 12:10
For they verily for a few days chastened us after their own pleasure; but he for our profit, that we might be partakers of his holiness.

Hebrews 13:1
Let brotherly love continue.

Hebrews 13:18
Pray for us: for we trust we have a good conscience, in all things willing to live honestly.

James 2:8
If ye fulfil the royal law according to the scripture, Thou shalt love thy neighbour as thyself, ye do well:

James 5:11
Behold, we count them happy which endure. Ye have heard of the patience of Job, and have seen the end of the Lord; that the Lord is very pitiful, and of tender mercy.

1 Peter 1:8
Whom having not seen, ye love; in whom, though now ye see him not, yet believing, ye rejoice with joy unspeakable and full of glory:

1 Peter 2:9
But ye are a chosen generation, a royal priesthood, an holy nation, a peculiar people; that ye should shew forth the praises of him who hath called you out of darkness into his marvellous light:

1 Peter 3:20
Which sometime were disobedient, when once the longsuffering of God waited in the days of Noah, while the ark was a preparing, wherein few, that is, eight souls were saved by water.

2 Peter 1:7
And to godliness brotherly kindness; and to brotherly kindness charity.

2 Peter 1:17
For He received from God the Father honour and glory, when there came such a voice to him from the excellent glory, this is my beloved son in whom I am well pleased

1 John 2:28
And now, little children, abide in him; that, when he shall appear, we may have confidence, and not be ashamed before him at his coming.

1 John 4:7
Beloved, let us love one another: for love is of God; and every one that loveth is born of God, and knoweth God.

1 John 5:4
For whatsoever is born of God overcometh the world: and this is the victory that overcometh the world, even our faith.

Revelation 3:19
As many as I love, I rebuke and chasten: be zealous therefore, and repent.

Revelation 15:2
And I saw as it were a sea of glass mingled with fire: and them that had gotten the victory over the beast, and over his image, and over his mark, and over the number of his name, stand on the sea of glass, having the harps of God.

Revelation 21:24
And the nations of them which are saved shall walk in the light of it: and the kings of the earth do bring their glory and honour into it.

Author's Notes

When I was in high school, I thought that I wanted to be a writer. I was told I could never be a writer because of my poor handwriting; it was worse than it is now and I had a fear of failure. My handwriting only improved a little; it became more legible but not enough for some people to read. My desire to write became stronger despite the opinion of others, and being very fearful that I would not succeed. When I graduated high school in '85, I still believed I would become a writer, but did not focus on it.

After I moved to Florida in '88 from Michigan, I finally started writing a book. I only told a few people whom I did not know very well that I was writing. None of them discouraged me; some of them said I could if I really wanted to do it. I quit writing my book after a year and a half because I could not get my book to make sense and I feared it would be rejected so I just worked at a job.

I started my next book in '90. I only wrote one page and stopped again. I thought I would want to wait until I was married and had more time to write so I put it off.

Then in '93 I began writing word puzzles. I wrote 8 pages with 2 puzzles per page. I did 3 pages of crosswords and word searches and two of word scrambles. I saved all my work in hopes I could do something with it later.

For 6 years I put off doing anything with it. My handwriting was just so bad to ever be a writer. I could not get myself to improve enough to do it or overcome my fear of failing. I did realize years later that if my books were typed, no one would know how messy my handwriting really is - except for my autograph when doing book signings. Despite my hand writing my ideas are interesting, which is more important when writing.

In '99 I prayed several times to God to know what I should do with my life. God's answer was to finish the puzzle books I started. I would reply, "No, I can't write books that can't be what I was meant to do." I would pray for another answer. The vision of what I was meant to do was to write books starting with the word puzzles I had wrote down. At first I kept saying my writing is so very sloppy that I thought it would not do good, God's answers stayed the same so I found the papers a few weeks later and I started to finish the books. When I got it to look like I wanted it to be, God said in the vision to finish it His way. I did not want to rewrite it, but was convinced to do the book again differently by separating the three kinds of puzzles into just one puzzle at a time starting with the word scramble alone rather than all together. God again said to do it His way; I did not want to revise the book again, but was convinced it would sell better if I did it. I rewrote it with the definition of the word with the verse and word.

When I had doubts during the writing, God would just say keep going and I would, and then after finishing it I looked for a publisher. I was led to someone who would publish it and we got it into print so I could sell my books.

I created this book by computer and published it with the help of a private publisher who helped me make it look more professional. The private publisher uses magazines with advertisements paid by sponsors, and does not need high volume magazine sales to earn money. My first publisher was unable to code books with a Library of Congress or ISBN so that the books may be sold in most bookstores. After it was in print I revised the word scramble again to have the definition closer to the meaning of each word in the Bible. After the next printing, a friend I have known for a long time helped the book look even better and we worked together to make the definition of each word even closer or right on to what it means in each verse. I started with a word and verse and went to a question of the word and verse..

My books are Bible study motivators – fun, interesting, challenging, educational, and self-benefiting. In the process of writing the books, I read the Bible and studied more for understanding of how words are used in verses, and how different words were used in the Biblical terms. I really do love and enjoy writing. It has given me more confidence in life.

I have sold more than 500 of my first book in just over a year. With my second puzzle book word search I have written, I've sold an additional 50 books in a year, My first book was priced very low at first, only $2.00 tax included. Each book was 32 pages, including 26 pages with letters from A to Z.

While writing the word scramble I started writing children's books. I finished my word scramble and got it into print as my first book. While writing the word search I started writing novels, I did the word search and got it in print as my second book. I traveled and found an illustrator for my children's book and got Counting with Animals self-published for my third book. While I was making the word search better I got the word scramble actually self-published with a ISBN and bar code and made it look even better. Later I started to write lyrics to songs for a songbook while writing the crossword puzzle. My song lyrics still needed editing and notes. I wasn't sure that I knew how I wanted the songs melody to sound. I do intend to write other books. I have finished the writing part of 6 children books before I got the main publisher, only needed editing and pictures I am no artist, so that could take awhile. I have taken a long time to be able to get my novels finished.

After I got my first book published with a ISBN and bar code was in print, I wanted to travel for selling my books. Within a year that my first book was in print, I made reservations to travel to promote my writings. I started with bookstores in my hometown of Ocala.

Most of my book sales were by word-of-mouth, door-to-door, and through consignment bookstores. I have traveled to sell books and really want to travel for book signings. I have sold a few books through consignments in bookstores. The first bookstore that accepted my book only sold a few every year, but is still selling books. The second bookstore sold two to five copies a month until it went out of business just over a year later.

The month my word scramble was self published I went with my parents over 500 to Key West and got my books in a bookstore there 3/2004. In April I traveled north with my editor Charles A. Schuman to Georgia as far Macon over 300 miles, and got in a bookstore there. The same month I went to Orlando around 100 miles away with my editor Charles A. Schuman and I got in a bookstore there.

I went with editor C.A.S. and got my books in a few stores in Volusia in May, less than 100 miles away. I went alone and got in bookstores in Alachua, next county north of Marion in August.

I lost my home from the hurricane Jeanne in 9/04. I still did two radio interviews 11/2004 and 12/04. In a radio interview about my first book, callers were challenged to solve a few of the puzzles from the book – winners were given a free copy of my book. I got in another store in Marion 12/04. I have tried many other stores and they would not take the books because they only take books from main publisher or distributors, and a few didn't take that kind of books.

I got books in a store in Kissimmee over 100 miles away in 2/2005, and then went with C.A.S. to Titusville over 200 miles in 3/2005. I did my first book signing in bookstore Marion County in 3/05. I got a new home in April the month of my Birthday. I traveled in 6/05 got in another store in Volusia. I went to Michigan with my Parents in July of 05 and got books in a store there the same city I was born Charlotte in Eaton County MI.

I improved my first book again for another printing and got my second book published with a ISBN in 12/05. I did my second book signing in Volusia in 12/05.

The next month and year I spoke on the Radio for another interview when I found out my books were advertise with online bookstores in 1/06. I have gotten into more bookstores by consignment and some bookstores paid me for the books. Now I only get into stores that pay for the books. I have done more and will do more book signings and radio interviews I started to work on doing interviews for the local newspaper and magazines, and do TV interviews. God Bless all of you.

God invites you to Heaven

Heaven is a perfect place. It is the land of promise, everyone is happy there. It is a place with a bright everlasting future. It is a land of love, giving, purity, and truth where no one is in any kind of pain. People don't mourn or die there. Jesus paid the price for the sins in our life when He gave His life, His body and His blood to make it possible for us to enter the kingdom of heaven.

Jesus came from Heaven to Earth as an act of mercy. Jesus Christ is a friend that loves and cares very much for you. He doesn't want you to be unhappy. He would like to give you something to have faith in other than the things of the world. All you need to do is to obey God by accepting the Lord as your friend and Saviour.

God offers you the opportunity to be born again. When you are born again the Holy Spirit comes to live inside of you. God would like everyone to join Him in Heaven but each person has a choice to make. The sooner you come to Jesus the sooner the world becomes brighter because once you belong to God you can shine his presence into the world. If you invite Jesus into your heart, God himself, creator of the universe, will be your father and your friend.

God offers all this, because he loves you! It is his gift to the people who were created in his image. It doesn't matter how badly you have sinned in the past. God offers you a second chance, in newness of life.

- John 3:16 - For God so loved the world, that he gave His only begotten Son, that whosoever believeth in him should not perish, but have everlasting life.
- Romans 3:23 - For we all have sinned and come short of the glory of God.
- Romans 5:8 - But God commendeth His Love toward us in that while we were yet sinners, Christ died for us.
- Romans 6:23 - For the wages of sin is death, but the gift of God is eternal life through Jesus Christ our Lord.
- Romans 10:9 - That if thou shalt confess with thy mouth the Lord Jesus, and shalt believe in thine heart that God hath raised Him from the dead, thou shalt be saved.

- Ephesians 2:8, 9 - For by grace are ye saved and that not of ourselves. It is the gift of God, not by works, lest anyone should boast.
- 1 John 5:14,15 - And this is the confidence that we have in him, that, if we ask any thing according to His will, he heareth us: And if we know that he hear us, whatsoever we ask, we know that we have the petitions that we desired of him.

Give yourself the chance to know God; and say this prayer and mean it from your heart:

Dear Heavenly Father, please change everything I am to what you want me to be. Make me a child of Heaven. Transform me from darkness to light. I ask you to give me your nature and your heart. I have sinned and I need a savior because I could never pay for my own sins. I believe that Jesus gave up His life to pay for my sins and He was raised from the dead so the same power can give me a new life. I ask for this new life. I ask you to put your spirit and your words inside me. Cause me to hear when you speak. Help me to know it is you when I hear you speak and help me to understand the bible. Jesus, Heavenly Father, Holy Spirit have your way in my life. Lead me to good people who know you and love you and will love me.

In Jesus name,
Amen. (which means: Let it be established)

If you prayed that prayer and meant it from your heart, God just granted what you asked because it is God's will for you to be born into His family. The Holy Spirit will be your constant companion and your guide.

Now watch for signs and miracles to follow. God will show you He is there, that He is real and that He cares for you in ways only He can. Obey the Holy Spirit and the bible and find a good church to help you grow in the Lord.

God bless you, in Jesus' name.

Amen!

Order Form

Name_____

Address _____

_____

Quantity _____   Book title_____
Word Puzzles of the Bible From A to Z Word Scramble
Price   _____
Total   _____

Marie Anne's House
Diane Bannard
P.O. Box 6788
Ocala FL. 34478
Phone #   352-598-5383

dianemarieba@yahoo.com

Comments _____

_____

CPSIA information can be obtained at www.ICGtesting.com
Printed in the USA
LVOW090814131111

254706LV00002BA/108/P